Minister's Simplified Filing System

Minister's Simplified Filing System

M. K. W. Heicher

BAKER BOOK HOUSE
Grand Rapids, Michigan

PHOTOLITHOPRINTED BY CUSHING - MALLOY, INC.
ANN ARBOR, MICHIGAN, UNITED STATES OF AMERICA
1976

FOREWORD

A filing system for ministers should be simple, be easy to use, yield the desired results. We believe that this system meets these requirements.

By using this system the desired illustration, the sermonic theme, the important quotation, the notes made in moments of inspiration, the pregnant facts will be at hand when needed.

This book should be as valuable to missionaries, Church School teachers, and other Church workers, as to ministers.

M. K. W. Heicher

CONTENTS

Foreword 5

Introductory Explanations

    Equipment Needed 9

    Procedure When Filing Clippings 9

    Procedure When Filing References
        from Books 10

    Multiple Filing 10

    Personal Papers and Writings 11

    Accumulation 11

    Reference 11

    Notes 12

Table No. I   Subjects in Alphabetical Order
             with Filing Numbers 13

Table No. II Subjects in Numerical Filing
             Order 55

Table III   Record of Sermons and
             Addresses 87

INTRODUCTORY EXPLANATIONS

Equipment Needed

1. A copy of this book.
2. Four to ten small drawers or divisions in a larger drawer. (The drawers used by the writer measure 10 inches by $8\frac{1}{2}$ inches, and 4 inches deep.) Boxes can be used instead.

   Supposing that four drawers are used to begin with, they are labeled 1-250; 250-499; 500-749; 750-1000.
3. Card-board boxes with lids. Begin with just a few. (The ones used by the writer are 11 inches by $7\frac{1}{2}$ inches, and 2 inches deep.)

   It is advantageous to have the boxes uniform in size and color, though this is not necessary. The number of these boxes will increase as the papers multiply.
4. A pair of scissors and a stapler.
5. Some small pads of paper for notes. The local printer is generally glad to supply these, made of waste cuttings, for a small price. $5\frac{1}{2}$ inches by 2 inches is a convenient size.

Procedure When Filing Clippings

1. Clip from the magazine or newspaper the article which you wish to keep.

2. Determine the subject under which you wish to file it. For example: "Courage," "Christmas," "Boy Scouts," etc.
3. Find the number of this subject in this book, Table I. Write this number upon the clipping. Check the subject in the book. The check-mark will tell you later that you have something filed under the subject or heading.
4. Place the clipping in the drawer which includes the number on the clipping.

Procedure When Filing References from Books

Illustration: Here are sentences to be found on page 108 of God Is Light by Edgar Primrose Dickie:

"Goodness without God may last a long time; but its roots are severed. It is only awaiting its end. It has no continuance . . ."

You may wish to refer to this again. Turn to Table I. Goodness is No. 301. Write the number 301 on the margin of Dickie's book. On one of the small slips write "301, Dickie, God Is Light, p. 108." File slip in 250-499 drawer. Check the word "Goodness" in Table I.

Multiple Filing

Illustration: In this same book, God Is Light, there is an anecdote taken from the writings of Miss Dorothy Canfield. It might be filed under the subjects "Courage," "Glory of

Man," "Childhood," and "War." Make out four slips: one numbered 297 for "Courage," one numbered 225 for "Glory of Man," one numbered 221 for "Childhood," and one 887 for "War"; each with the notation "Dickie, God Is Light, p. 118." The numbers were secured from Table I.

Write the numbers opposite the reference in Dickie's book. File slips in drawers according to their numbers. Check the subjects in Table I.

Suppose that a clipping filed under "Goodness, No. 301" might also be valuable if filed under "Community Life, No. 820." A slip may be made out and filed as follows: "820, See 301, Clipping from . . ."

Personal Papers and Writings

These can be handled in the same way as clippings. The stapler may be used to fasten sheets together, or if more convenient envelopes may be used.

Accumulation

Illustration: Suppose that many clippings and references accumulate under No. 782, "Easter." The drawer 750-1000 begins to fill up. Now is the time to transfer all 782's to one of the card-board boxes, which is now given the number 782. Important subjects will gradually find their way to boxes.

Reference

Illustration: Suppose that you wish material under "Christmas." Reference to Table I finds "Christmas" as 766. You discover that "Christmas" has been checked; material has been filed. All slips numbered 766 can quickly be removed from the file to be looked over. Those not used can be returned; as can also those which have been used, with use noted on a slip stapled to the clipping.
If "Christmas" rates a box, taken to your desk it may yield up great treasure.

Notes

See Table I "EXTRA NUMBERS," after Z, for paragraph concerning subjects not listed in Table I.
In Table II the indentations do not indicate that the indented items are sub-heads or sub-subjects. In some cases they are, but not always. The indentations move from the general to the particular, but this is only roughly so. It will be noted that subjects which are more or less related have a tendency to be near each other by number. This proves to be a factor of advantage.

A textual reference would be filed under the heading of the book on the Bible in which it is found.

Table III is added for recording the sermons prepared by the user of the book.

TABLE I

Subjects in Alphabetical Order
with Filing Numbers

TABLE NO. I

Subjects in Alphabetical Order
with Filing Numbers

A

Accounts   963
Acts of the Apostles   70
Administration of Church   504
Administration of Church School or Sunday School   475
Administration of Justice, Relation of Church to   410
Administration of Laws   858
Admission of Members   467
Adolescence   222
Adoption of Christianity by Rome   622
Adult Delinquency   370
Adult Education   408
Adult Religious Education   481
Advent, Church Year   765
Adventist Churches   659
Advent of Christ   136
Advocate, Holy Spirit as   208
Aesthetics   431
Africa   572
Agapé   276
Aged in Family   234
Age, Gerontology   377
Agricultural Missions   599
Aids for Church School or Sunday School   479
Aids to Worship   452

Alcoholics Anonymous   718
Alcoholism   395
All Saints' Day   806
Altar, Family   345
Altruism   821
Anabaptists   630
Ancestor Worship   903
Ancient Controversies   623
Angels   249
Animals, Kindness to   854
Animism   902
Anniversaries   745
Anthems   459
American Citizenship   827
American Council of Christian Churches   725
Amos   54
Apocrypha   98
Apologetics   258
Apostles   613
Apostolic Churches   614
Apostolic Missions   547
April   754
Archaeology, Biblical   102
Archaeology, Christian   102
Architecture, Church   426
Armistice Day   812
Ascension Day   789
Ascension of Christ   151
Asia, Southeastern   557
Aspiration   293
Assemblies of God   662
Assurance   272
Athletics   521
Atom Bomb   822
Atonement, The   161

Attendance at Church 539
Attributes of Christ 186
Attributes of God 110
Audio-Visual Aids 451
August 758
Australia, Church in 733
Authors of Hymns 456
Autumn 748
Awe 323

B

Baptism 465
Baptist Churches 665
Baptism of Christ 138
Baptism of the Holy Spirit 210
Beauty 431
Benedictions 448
Benevolence 300
Bereaved 501
Betrothal 342
Bible Institutes and Bible Colleges 486
Bible Manuscripts 19
Bible Societies 104
Bible Sunday 814
Bible, The 17
Bible Versions 18
Biblical Atchaeology 102
Bill of Rights 833
Biographies 929
Biography of (Write in) 930
Biography of 931
Biography of 932
Biography of 933
Biography of 934

Bulletin Board 530
Bulletin Board Slogans 531
Bulletin, Church 436
Burial of Dead 472
Business Letters 961
Business, Relation of Church to 400

C

Calendar, Church 436
Call, Sense of Vocation 267
Calls to Worship 439
Calmness 325
Calvinistic Reformation 631
Campaigns, Financial 511
Camps, Summer 515
Canada 823
Canadian Churches 727
Canvass, Financial 510
Capitalism 824
Care of the Aged 825
Care of the Mentally Ill 863
Catechisms 257
Chants 459
Charity 275
Chastity 319
Cheerfulness 311
Childhood 221
Childhood of Christ 137
Child Nurture and Care 355
Child Psychology 354
Children 221
Children of God 287
Children's Day 792
China 561

Choir   460
Christ, His Life   134
Christian and Missionary Alliance   672
Christian Education   473
Christian Education Week   801
Christian Home Sunday   785
Christian Life, The   261
Christian Literature, Early   620
Christian Reformed Church in America   673
Christian Science   715
Christian Unity Sunday   793
Christian Virtues   292
Christmas   766
Christology   154
Chronicles I   34
Chronicles II   35
Church Administration   504
Church and Home Relationship   347
Church and Political Action   873
Church and State   411
Church and State in the National Life   826
Church Attendance   539
Church Co-operation   720
Church Doctrines   424
Churches of God   662
Church Fathers   621
Church Finance   508
Church Government   423
Church of the Nazarene   684
Church Organization   504
Church Polity   423
Church Publicity   529
Church Records   507
Church School   474
Church Statistics   535

Church, The   383
Church Triumphant   489
Church Union   720
Church Union on Mission Fields   596
Citizenship, American   827
City Church, The   537
City Missions   594
Civilization   828
Clergy   491
Clippings, Local Church   647
Clippings of Personal Interest   967
Clubs, Interest   520
Colleges   842
Colleges, The Church and   404
Colossians   78
Comforter, Holy Spirit as   208
Commencement Sunday   791
Communion of Saints   489
Communion, The   464
Communism   829
Communism, Relation of Church to   387
Community Churches   674
Community Life   820
Compassion   296
Compassion of Christ   187
Compassion of God   111
Composers of Hymns   457
Conduct   228
Conferences, Summer   515
Confessions   255
Confidence   271
Confucianism   910
Congregational-Christian Church   676
Congregational Churches   675
Conscience   330

Conscientious Objectors   888
Consecration   294
Consolation   502
Constitution of the United States   832
Contentment   317
Contrition   295
Controversies, Ancient   623
Conversion   230
Conversion, Examples of   231
Conversion, The Christian Life   264
Corinthians I   73
Corinthians I:13   97
Corinthians II   74
Council of Churches, Local   724
Council of Churches, National   722
Council of Churches, Regional   723
Counselling, Pastoral   503
Counter-Reformation   634
Courage   297
Courts   413
Courtship   341
Covenants, Creedal   256
Covenants of Fellowship   290
Covetousness   236
Creator, Christ as   156
Creator, God the   107
Creeds   254
Cross, The   160
Crucifixion of Christ   149
Crusades   626
Cults   717
Cultural Conditions, Greek   100
Cultural Conditions, Hebrew   99
Cultural Conditions, Roman   101
Curriculum and Aids, Church School or Sunday
    School   476

D

Daniel   51
Day of Prayer for Students   776
Days, Special   744
Dead Sea Scrolls   103
Death   378
Death of Christ   149
Decalogue, The   39
December   762
Declaration of Independence   834
Dedication   294
Dedication of Children   466
Dedications of Buildings, Organs, etc.   470
Delinquency of Adults   370
Delinquency of Children   368
Delinquency of Youth   369
Delinquents, Ministry to   499
Democracy   835
Democracy, Relation of Church to   386
Demons   250
Denominational Histories   637
Denominational Statistics   743
Denominations   652
Dependability   299
Depravity   226
Deuteronomy   26
Devils   250
Devotion   294
Diligence   298
Diplomacy, The Church and   418
Discipleship   266
Disciples of Christ (Denomination)   677
Discipline, Family   363
Divine Service   435

Divinity of Christ   157
Divorce and the Community   839
Divorce and the Family   371
Doctrine of The Church   422
Dominion of Man   223
Door, Christ the   180
Doubt   237
Dreams   227
Drinking   861
Dunkers   669
Duty   268

E

Early Christian Literature   620
Early Church Missions   548
Early European Missions   549
Early Missionary Societies   552
Earnestness   298
Earnestness of Christ   197
Easter   782
Eastern Orthodox Churches   657
Ecclesiastes   44
Ecclesiology   430
Economics and Religion   8
Ecumenicity   720
Education   840
Educational Missions   600
Education in Sacred Music   488
Education of Children   364
Education, Relation of Church to   402
Election Sunday   811
England, Churches in   728
English Reformation   632
Ephesians   76

Episcopal Churches   678
Epistles   71
Equipment of Church   427
Era of Modern Denominationalism   636
Eschatology   252
Esther   38
Eternal Life, Christian Experience of   336
Eternal Life, Future State   253
Eternity of God   112
Ethical Societies   717
Ethics   864
Ethics of Sex   232
Eucharist, The   464
Europe   584
Evangelical and Reformed Church   679
Evangelical and United Brethren Church   680
Evangelism   512
Evangelistic Missions   601
Evening   764
Evidences of Christianity   258
Exaltation of Christ   162
Example   309
Example of Christ   185
Examples of Conversion   231
Exodus   23
Expectation of Life   860
Experience of Man   235
Ezekiel   50
Ezra   36

F

Faith   271
Faithfulness   299
Faithfulness of God   113

Faith Missions 602
Family 340
Family Altar 345
Family Interests 984
Family Night 449
Family Week 784
Family Worship 345
Fatherhood, Family 349
Fatherhood, Manhood 219
Fatherhood of God 129
Fathers, Church 621
Father's Day 795
Favor of God 116
Fear 238
February 752
Fellowship 286
Fellowship, Organizations for 522
Fellowship with Christ 288
Fidelity 299
Finance, Church 508
Financial Campaigns 511
Financial Canvass 510
First Century Churches 614
Flag Day 796
Flag, The 796
Forbearance 296
Forefathers' Day 815
Forgiveness 262
Forgiveness, Christ's Spirit of 195
Fraternal Orders 849
Freedom 859
Friendship 291
Friends, Societies of 681
Fun 376
Funerals 379

Furnishings of Church   428
Future State   253

G

Galatians   75
Gambling   852
Games   375
Genealogy of Jesus   135
General Organizations   523
Generosity   300
Genesis   22
Gerontology   825
Girl Scouts   407
Girls' Organizations   528
Giving   282
Gladness   311
Glory of God   114
Glory of Man   225
God   105
Golden Rule   96
Good Friday   781
Goodness   301
Goodness of God   115
Goodness of Man   225
Good Shepherd, The   181
Gospels and Acts   65
Government, Relation of Church to   410
Grace at Table   346
Grace of God   116
Grace of Holy Spirit   215
Grace, Virtue   302
Gratitude   303
Greatness   304
Greatness of Man   225

Great Things   333
Greco-Roman Civilization (Bible Times)   611
Greek Cultural Conditions (Bible Times)   100
Greek Social Conditions (Bible Times)   100
Guidance   278

H

Habakkuk   59
Habits   229
Haggai   61
Happiness   359
Healing by Christ   143
Health   233
Health in Family   367
Hebrew Cultural Conditions (Bible Times)   99
Hebrews, Epistle to   83
Hebrew Social Conditions (Bible Times)   99
Heresies   619
Heroism   225
Hinayana Buddhism   907
Hinduism   904
Histories, Denominational   637
Historical Books of Old Testament   21
History, Christian Interpretation of   6
History of Missions   546
History of the Christian Church   610
Hobbies   954
Holiness   305
Holiness Churches   683
Holiness of Christ   189
Holiness of God   117
Holland, Churches of   732
Holy Ghost, The   207
Holy Spirit, The   207

Holy Week 778
Home 340
Home and Church Relationship 347
Home and Community Relationship 368
Home and School Relationship 365
Home-making 356
Home Missions 590
Home Problems 372
Homiletics 490
Honesty 310
Honor 306
Hope 273
Hosea 52
Hospitality 307
Hospitals 853
Hospitals and Healing 397
Humane Societies 854
Humanism and Reformation 628
Humanitarianism, Relation of Church to 394
Humanity of Christ 158
Humility 308
Humility of Christ 190
Humor 240
Hymn Books 458
Hymnology 454
Hymns 455

I

Ideals 227
Idolatry 917
Images of Christ 206
Immortality 253
Immutability of God 118
Income Tax 855

Income Tax, Estimates   973
Income Tax, Personal   969
Income Tax Returns, Current   972
Income Tax Returns, Last Year's   971
Income Tax Returns, Old   970
Independence Day   797
India   555
Individualism   362
Industry   856
Industry, Relation of Church to   400
Infinity of God   119
Influence   309
Influence of Church   384
Iniquity   226
Inspiration of the Holy Spirit   209
Installations   469
Institutional Work   516
Integrity   310
Intercession   270
Intercessor, The   169
Interest Clubs   520
Interests, Family   360
Interests, Personal   978
International Affairs, Relation of Church to   416
International Life   820
International Missionary Organizations   542
Introits   459
Invisibility of God   120
Invocations   440
Isaiah   47
Islam   914

J

Jainism 905

James, Epistle of 84

January 751

Japan 562

Jeremiah 48

Jesus, the Christ 133

Jewish Life and Thought (Bible Times) 612

Jews, Missions to 604

Job 41

Joel 53

John, Gospel of 69

John I, Epistle of 87

John II, Epistle of 88

John III, Epistle of 89

Jonah 56

Joshua 27

Joy 311

Jude, Epistle of 90

Judge, Christ as 177

Judges, Book of 28

July 757

June 756

Justice 312

Justice of Christ 188

Justice of God 115

Justification 262

K

Kindness 296

Kindness to Animals 854

King, Christ as 175

Kingdom of Christ 163

Kingdom of God   337
Kings I   32
Kings II   33
Korea   563

L

Labor   857
Labor Movement, Relation of Church to   401
Labor Sunday   798
Labor Unions   857
Lamaism   909
Lamentations, Book of   49
Last Things   252
Latter Day Saints   716
Latin America   577
Law   858
Laymen, Responsibilities of   505
Laymen's Missionary Movement   545
Laymen's Sunday   803
Leaders, Missionary   608
Legislation, The Church and   415
Leisure   241
Lent   768
Lepers, Missions to   605
Letters   959
Letters, Business   961
Letters, Local Church   649
Letters, Personal   960
Leviticus, Book of   24
Liberty   859
Library of Church   482
Life   860
Life, Christ the   182
Life of Christ   134

Light of God   114
Light of the World, The   179
Lincoln's Birthday   775
Liquor Traffic   861
Lists of Local Church   646
Litanies   442
Literature and Religion   12
Literature, Missionary   609
Literature, Relation of Church to   390
Little Things   332
Liturgies   435
Local Church Clippings   647
Local Church History   643
Local Church Letters   649
Local Church Lists   646
Local Church Photographs   648
Local Church Publications   645
Local Church Records   644
Local Council of Churches   724
Lodges   849
Logos, The   172
Lord's Day, The   434
Lord's Prayer, The   95
Lord's Supper, The   464
Love   274
Love, Family   357
Love of Christ   191
Love of God   121
Lovingkindness of God   121
Loyalty   313
Loyalty, Family   358
Loyalty Sunday   799
Luke, Gospel of   68
Lutheran Churches   687
Lutheran Reformation   629
Luxury   862

M

Magazine Articles 953
Mahayana Buddhism 908
Maintenance of Church Buildings 506
Majesty of God 114
Malachi 63
Man, His Dominion 223
Man, His Works 223
Manhood 219
Man, Personality of 218
Manuscripts of Bible 19
Maps 976
March 753
Mark, Gospel of 67
Marriage 343
Martyrs 617
Matthew, Gospel of 66
Maundy Thursday 780
May 755
Mediaeval Church 625
Mediator, The 169
Medical Missions 603
Medical Science and Religion 5
Meditation 277
Meekness of Christ 192
Memorial Day 788
Mennonite Churches 691
Men's Organizations 524
Mentally Ill 863
Mercy 314
Mercy of God 121
Messiah, The 167
Methodist Churches 693
Methods for Church School or Sunday School 478
Methods, Missions 598

Micah   57
Middle Ages, Missions   550
Mid-week Service   449
Ministry   491
Ministry of Christ   141
Ministry to Bereaved   501
Ministry to Delinquents   499
Ministry to Sick   500
Miracles   93
Miracles of Christ   142
Miscellaneous   950
Missionary Education   483
Missionary Leaders   608
Missionary Literature   609
Missionary Methods   598
Missionary Outlook   597
Missionary Societies and Movements   544
Missionary Statistics   554
Missionary Sunday   783
Missionary Training   607
Mission Covenant Church of America, Evangelical
   699
Mission Fields   554
Mission Fields, Church Union on   596
Mission of Christ   140
Missions   541
Missions, Apostolic   547
Missions, City   594
Missions, Early Church   548
Missions, Early European   549
Missions, Early Missionary Societies   552
Missions, History of   546
Missions, Modern   553
Missions, Orphaned   589
Missions, Period of the Middle Ages   550

Missions, Period of the Reformation   551
Missions, Statistics   554
Missions, Stories   554
Missions to Jews   604
Missions to Lepers   605
Missions to Seamen   606
Modern Denominationalism, Era of   636
Modern Missions   553
Mohammedanism   914
Mongolian Buddhism   909
Morality   864
Moral Rearmament Movement   719
Morals, Civilization, Relation of Church to   385
Moravian Church   700
Mormons   716
Morning   763
Motherhood, Relation to Race   220
Motherhood, Relation to Family   350
Mother's Day   786
Motion Pictures, Relation of Church to   391
Music, Sacred   454

N

Nahum   58
Names of Christ   202
Narcotics   865
Narcotics, Use of   396
National Council of Churches   722
Nationalism   866
National Life   820
National Missions   590
National Mores, Relation of Church to   389
Nature   13
Near East   568

Nehemiah   37
Neighborhood Houses   519
New Birth   264
Newspaper Publicity   534
New Testament   64
New Year   767
New Zealand, Church in   734
Non-Christian Cults   916
Non-Christian Philosophies   901
Non-Christian Religions   901
North America, Missions   590
Norway, Churches in   730
November   761
Numbers, Book of   25

O

Obadiah   55
Obedience   315
Obedience of Christ   193
October   760
Offertory Prayers   445
Offertory Sentences   444
Old Age   234
Old Testament   20
Omnipotence of God   122
Omnipresence of God   123
Omniscience of God   124
Optimism   311
Orchestra   461
Order of Service   436
Ordinances   463
Ordination   468
Organization of Church   504
Organizations for Boys   527

Organizations for Fellowship 522
Organizations for Girls 528
Organizations for Men 524
Organizations for Parish Work 522
Organizations for Welfare Work 522
Organizations for Women 525
Organizations for Young People 526
Organizations, General 523
Organs 429
Orphaned Missions 589
Outlook on Mission Fields 597

P

Pacific Islands 564
Pakistan 556
Palm Sunday 779
Papacy 624
Parables 94
Parables of Christ 146
Paraclete, Holy Spirit as 208
Parental Responsibility 351
Parish Missions 513
Parish Paper 533
Parish Work, Organizations for 522
Parochial Schools 845
Parsees 913
Passion of Christ 148
Pastoral Counselling 503
Pastoral Responsibility 348
Pastoral Work 498
Patience 316
Patriotism 867
Peace, International 868
Peace Movements 870

Peace Sunday   810
Peace, The Church and   420
Peace, Virtue   317
Pensions   871
Pentecost   790
Pentecostal Churches   662
Perfection   305
Perfection of God   125
Persecutions, Early Church   616
Personality   218
Personal Letters   960
Personal Matters   950
Personal Religion   338
Pessimism   239
Peter I, Epistle of   85
Peter II, Epistle of   86
Philanthropics, Relation of Church to   394
Philippians, Epistle to   77
Philosophy and Religion   2
Philosophy of Religion   3
Photographs, Local Church   648
Photographs of Personal Interest   968
Pictures of Christ   206
Play   242
Play in the Home   373
Plymouth Brethren   701
Poetic Books of the Old Testament   40
Poetry, Religious   462
Political Action, The Church and   873
Political Parties   872
Politics   872
Politics, Relation of Church to   410
Poverty   874
Power   318
Power of Christ   194

Power of God 122
Power of the Holy Spirit 211
Praise 303
Prayer 270
Prayer-books 453
Prayermeeting 449
Prayers of Christ 147
Prayers, Pastoral 443
Prayers with Choir 438
Preaching in Worship 447
Preaching, The Art of 492
Pre-existence of Christ 155
Preparation for Christianity, Greco-Roman 611
Preparation for Christianity, Jewish Life and
   Thought 612
Presbyterian Churches 702
Presence of Christ 201
Presence of God 123
Presence of the Holy Spirit 212
Preserver, God the 108
Press, The 875
Priest, Christ as 174
Primitive Peoples, Religion of 902
Prince of Peace, The 176
Prisons and Crime 414
Profanity 876
Programs, Church 436
Progress 877
Promises of Christ 200
Prophet, Christ as 173
Prophetic Books of the Old Testament 46
Protestant Episcopal Church 678
Protestantism 658
Protestant Reformation 627
Protestant Revolution 627

Proverbs, Book of   43
Providence, God   106
Psalms   42
Pseudepigrapha   98
Psychiatry   245
Psychiatry and Religion   11
Psycho-analysis   243
Psychology   244
Psychology and Religion   9
Psychology of Children   354
Psychology of Religion   10
Publications of Local Church   645
Publicity of Church   529
Public Schools   843
Public Schools, The Church and the   405
Purity   319
Purpose   320

Q

Quakers, The   706
Quietness   317

R

Race Problems   399
Race Relations   878
Race Relations Sunday   773
Radio, Relation of Church to   392
Rally Day   800
Receipts   964
Reception of Members   467
Reconciliation   265
Records, Local Church   644
Records of Church   507

Recreation and Play   373
Red Cross, Relation of Church to   398
Red Cross, National and International   880
Redeemer, The   168
Reformation, Calvinistic   631
Reformation, English   632
Reformation in Various Lands   633
Reformation, Lutheran   629
Reformation Period of Missions   551
Reformation, Protestant   627
Reformation Sunday   807
Reformed Church in America   708
Regeneration   213
Regional Council of Churches   723
Reign of Christ   203
Relation of Christ to the Father   159
Relation of Home to Community   368
Relation of Home to School   365
Relief, Relation of Church to   394
Religion and Nature   13
Religion in General   1
Religion in the Public Schools   844
Religious Art   433
Religious Drama   450
Religious Wars   635
Repentance   263
Replies to Letters   962
Resignation   321
Responsibilities of Laymen   505
Responsibility   322
Responsive Readings   441
Rest   317
Resurrection   335
Resurrection, Christ the   182
Resurrection of Christ   150

-42-

Retreats 514
Revelation of God 131
Revelation, The Book of 91
Reverence 323
Revivals 513
Revolution, Protestant 627
Righteousness 301
Righteousness of Christ 189
Righteousness of God 115
Ritual 435
Rituals, Special 463
Roman Catholicism 653
Romance and Courtship 341
Roman Cultural Conditions, Bible Times 101
Roman Empire and Christianity 615
Romans, Epistle to 72
Roman Social Conditions, Bible Times 101
Rural Church 536
Rural Life Sunday 787
Ruth, The Book of 29

S

Sabbath 434
Sacraments 463
Sacred Music 454
Sacred Music, Education in 488
Salvation 248
Salvation Army 713
Samuel I 30
Samuel II 31
Sanctification 214
Satan 251
Saviour, The 168
Science and Religion 4

Scotland, Church in   729
Seamen. Missions to   606
Seasons   744
Second Coming of Christ   164
Sects   717
Sects, Systems, Parties, in the Roman Empire
   618
Secularism   881
Segregation   879
Segregation of Races   399
Self-denial   324
Self-sacrifice   324
September   759
Serenity   325
Sermonic Literature   497
Sermon on the Mount   92
Sermons   493
Sermons of Others   495
Sermons, Original   494
Sermon Texts and Themes   496
Service   269
Sex Education   409
Sexual Ethics   232
Shinto   912
Sick, Ministry to   500
Sikhism   915
Silence in Worship   446
Simplicity   327
Sincerity   326
Sinfulness   226
Slogans for Bulletin Board   531
Social Conditions, Greek, Bible Times   100
Social Conditions, Hebrew, Bible Times   99
Social Conditions, Roman, Bible Times   101
Socialism   882

Socialism, Relation of Church to   388
Social Justice   883
Social Movements, Relation of Church to   394
Social Problems, Relation of Church to   394
Social Security   885
Social Security Papers   974
Social Service   884
Societies of Friends   681
Sociology and Religion   7
Solemnization of Matrimony   471
Song of Solomon, The   45
Son of God   170
Son of Man   171
Soteriology   248
South Africa, Church in   735
Southeastern Asia   557
Sovereignty of Christ   163
Sovereignty of God   128
Spirit of Forgiveness, Christ's   195
Spring   746
State and Church   411
Statistics, Church   535
Statistics, Denominational   743
Statistics of Mentally Ill   863
Stewardship   280
Stewardship of Talent   284
Stewardship of Time   283
Stewardship of Wealth   285
Stewardship Sunday   808
Stories from Mission Fields   554
Strength   328
Suburban Church   538
Sufferings of Christ   148
Summer   747
Summer Camps   515

Summer Conferences   515
Sunday   434
Sunday Calendar, Publicity   532
Sunday School   474
Superstition   918
Sweden, Churches in   731
Symbolism   432
Sympathy   296
Sympathy of Christ   187

T

Table Grace   346
Tact   228
Talent, Stewardship of   284
Taoism   911
Taxation   855
Teaching, Church School or Sunday School   477
Teaching of Christ   144
Television, Relation of Church to   393
Temperance Education   484
Temperance Movement   861
Temperance Sunday   809
Temptation   329
Temptation of Christ   139
Ten Commandments, The   39
Texts   496
Thanksgiving   303
Thanksgiving Day   813
Themes   496
Theological Education   485
Theological Seminaries   487
Thessalonians I, Epistle to   79
Thessalonians II, Epistle to   80
Tibetan Buddhism   909

Time, Stewardship of   283
Timothy I, Epistle to   81
Timothy II, Epistle to   82
Tithing   281
Titles of Christ   202
Training of Missionaries   607
Travel Notes   975
Trinity Sunday   794
Trinity, The   109
Trust   272
Truth   331
Truth, Christ the   183

U

Unchangeableness of God   118
Unitarian Church   709
United Brethren Church   680
United Nations   886
United Nations, The Church and   417
United Nations Week   804
United States of America   832
Unity of God   125
Universalist Church   710
Universities   841
Universities, The Church and the   403
Use of Narcotics   865
Ushering   437

V

Vacation   750
Vacation of Family   374
Vacation Church Schools   480
Values   331

Values, Family   361
Versions of the Bible   18
Veterans' Day   812
Victory   279
Vine, Christ the   184
Visions   227
Vocation   267
Vocational Education   846
Vocation, Sense of   224
Voice of God   132
Volunteers of America   714

W

War   887
Wars, Religious   635
War, The Church and   419
Washington's Birthday   777
Watch Night   816
Way, Christ the   183
Way, Truth, Life; Christ the   183
Wealth   889
Wealth, Stewardship of   285
Weddings   344
Wedding Services   471
Week of Prayer   770
Welfare   890
Welfare Work, Organizations for   522
Whitsunday   790
Winter   749
Wisdom of Christ   196
Wisdom of God   124
Witness   269
Witness of the Holy Spirit   212
Womanhood   220

Women's Organizations 525
Word, The 172
Work 269
Work of Christ 141
Works of God 130
Works of Man 223
World Council of Churches 721
World Day of Prayer 769
World Order Day 805
World Peace 869
World Temperance Sunday 809
World-Wide Communion Sunday 802
Worry 239
Worship 435
Worship, Family 345
Writings, Personal 977

Y

Year, Seasons, Days 744
Younger Churches, The 554
Y. M. C. A. 517
Young People's Organizations 526
Y. W. C. A. 518
Youth 222
Youth of Christ 137
Youth Sunday 772
Youth Week 771

Z

Zeal 298
Zeal of Christ 197
Zechariah 62
Zephaniah 60
Zoroastrianism 913

EXTRA NUMBERS

No list of subjects, unless unabridged, would perfectly meet the needs of all users of this book. The following numbers give opportunity for write-ins of subjects other than those given, thus increasing the use and value of the book. By reference to Table II it may be possible to choose a number for each write-in that will fit into the general scheme. It will be of advantage to write in the subjects in both tables using the corresponding numbers.

14
15
16
126
127
152
153
165
166
198
199
204
205
216
217
246
247
259
260
380
381
382

740
741
742
817
818
819
830
831
836
837
838
847
848
850
851
891
892
893
894
895
896
897
898
899
900
919
920
921
922
923
924
925
926
927
928

955
956
957
958
965
966
979
980
981
982
983
985
986
987
988
989
990
991
992
993
994
995
996
997
998
999
1000

TABLE II

Subjects in Numerical Filing Order

TABLE NO. II

Subjects in Numerical Filing Order

1. Religion in General
  2. Philosophy and Religion
    3. The Philosophy of Religion
  4. Science and Religion
    5. Religion and Medical Science
  6. The Christian Interpretation of History
  7. Sociology and Religion
    8. Economics and Religion
  9. Psychology and Religion
    10. The Psychology of Religion
  11. Psychiatry and Religion
  12. Religion and Literature
  13. Nature, Religion and Nature
  14.
  15.
  16.
17. Bible
    18. Versions of the Bible
    19. Manuscripts of the Bible
  20. Old Testament
    21. Historical Books
      22. Genesis
      23. Exodus
      24. Leviticus
      25. Numbers
      26. Deuteronomy
      27. Joshua
      28. Judges
      29. Ruth

30. I Samuel
31. II Samuel
32. I Kings
33. II Kings
34. I Chronicles
35. II Chronicles
36. Ezra
37. Nehemiah
38. Esther
39. Ten Commandments
40. Poetic Books
41. Job
42. Psalms
43. Proverbs
44. Ecclesiastes
45. Song of Solomon
46. Prophetic Books
47. Isaiah
48. Jeremiah
49. Lamentations
50. Ezekiel
51. Daniel
52. Hosea
53. Joel
54. Amos
55. Obadiah
56. Jonah
57. Micah
58. Nahum
59. Habakkuk
60. Zephaniah
61. Haggai
62. Zechariah
63. Malachi
64. New Testament

65. Gospels and Acts
    66. Matthew
    67. Mark
    68. Luke
    69. John
    70. Acts
71. Epistles
    72. Romans
    73. I Corinthians
    74. II Corinthians
    75. Galatians
    76. Ephesians
    77. Philippians
    78. Colossians
    79. I Thessalonians
    80. II Thessalonians
    81. I Timothy
    82. II Timothy
    83. Hebrews
    84. James
    85. I Peter
    86. II Peter
    87. I John
    88. II John
    89. III John
    90. Jude
91. Revelation
    92. Sermon on the Mount
    93. Miracles
    94. Parables
    95. The Lord's Prayer
    96. The Golden Rule
    97. I Corinthians 13
98. Apocrypha and Pseudepigrapha
    99. Hebrew Cultural and Social Conditions

100. Greek Cultural and Social Conditions

101. Roman Culture and Social Conditions

102. Biblical Archaeology

       103. Dead Sea Scrolls

104. Bible Societies

105. God

    106. Providence

    107. Creator

    108. Preserver

    109. The Trinity

        110. Attributes

           111. Compassion

           112. Eternity

           113. Faithfulness

           114. Glory, Majesty, Light

           115. Goodness, Righteousness, Justice

           116. Grace, Favor of God

           117. Holiness

           118. Immutability, Unchangeableness

           119. Infinity

           120. Invisibility

           121. Love, Mercy, Lovingkindness

           122. Omnipotence, Power

           123. Omnipresence, Presence

           124. Omniscience, Wisdom

           125. Unity, Perfection

           126.

           127.

    128. Sovereignty of God

    129. Fatherhood of God

       130. Works of God

131. Revelation of God
132. Voice of God
133. Jesus, the Christ
134. Life of Christ
135. Genealogy of Christ
136. Advent and Birth of Christ
137. Childhood and Youth of Christ
138. Baptism of Christ
139. Temptation of Christ
140. Mission of Christ
141. Ministry of Christ, Work of Christ
142. Miracles of Christ
143. Healings by Christ
144. Teaching of Christ
145. Sermon on the Mount
146. Parables of Christ
147. Prayers of Christ
148. Sufferings of Christ, Passion of Christ
149. Crucifixion of Christ, Death of Christ
150. Resurrection of Christ
151. Ascension of Christ
152.
153.
154. Christology
155. Pre-existence
156. Creator
157. Divinity
158. Humanity
159. Relation to the Father
160. The Cross
161. The Atonement
162. Exaltation of Christ

163. Sovereignty of Christ, Kingdom of Christ, Reign of Christ
164. Second Coming of Christ
165.
166.
167. Messiah
168. Saviour, Redeemer
169. Mediator, Intercessor
170. Son of God
171. Son of Man
172. The Word, Logos
173. Prophet
174. Priest
175. King
176. Prince of Peace
177. Judge
178. The Bread of Life
179. The Light of the World
180. The Door
181. The Good Shepherd
182. The Resurrection and the Life
183. The Way, the Truth, and the Life
184. The Vine
185. Example of Christ
186. Attributes of Christ
187. Compassion of Christ, Sympathy of Christ
188. Justice of Christ
189. Holiness of Christ, Righteousness of Christ
190. Humility of Christ
191. Love of Christ
192. Meekness of Christ
193. Obedience of Christ
194. Power of Christ

195. Christ's Spirit of Forgiveness
196. Wisdom of Christ
197. Zeal of Christ, Earnestness of Christ
198.
199.
200. Promises of Christ
201. Presence of Christ
202. Names and Titles of Christ
203. Reign of Christ
204.
205.
206. Pictures and Images of Christ
207. Holy Spirit, Holy Ghost
208. Comforter, Advocate, Paraclete
209. Inspiration of the Holy Spirit
210. Baptism of the Holy Spirit
211. Power of the Holy Spirit
212. Presence and Witness of the Holy Spirit
213. Regeneration
214. Sanctification
215. Grace
216.
217.
218. Man, Personality
219. Manhood, Fatherhood
220. Womanhood, Motherhood
221. Children, Childhood
222. Youth, Adolescence
223. Works of Man, Dominion of Man
224. Sense of Vocation
225. Goodness, Greatness, Glory, Heroism of Man
226. Depravity, Sinfulness, Iniquity

227. Ideals, Dreams, Visions
228. Conduct, Courtesy, Tact
    229. Habits
    230. Conversion
    231. Conversion, Examples of
232. Sexual Ethics
233. Health
234. Age, Gerontology
235. Experience
    236. Covetousness
    237. Doubt
    238. Fear
    239. Worry, Pessimism
    240. Humor
    241. Leisure
    242. Play
243. Psycho-analysis
244. Psychology
245. Psychiatry
246.
247.
248. Salvation, Soteriology
249. Angels
    250. Devils, Demons
      251. Satan
252. Last Things, Eschatology
253. Future State, Eternal Life, Immortality
254. Creeds
    255. Confessions
    256. Covenants
    257. Catechisms
258. Apologetics, Evidences of Christianity
    259.
    260.
261. The Christian Life

262. Forgiveness, Justification

263. Repentance

264. Conversion, New Birth

265. Reconciliation

266. Discipleship

    267. Vocation, Call

    268. Duty

    269. Work, Service, Witness

    270. Prayer, Intercession

    271. Faith, Confidence

    272. Trust, Assurance

    273. Hope

    274. Love

        275. Charity

        276. Agapé

    277. Meditation

    278. Guidance

    279. Victory

280. Stewardship

    281. Tithing

    282. Giving

    283. Time, Stewardship of

    284. Talent, Stewardship of

    285. Wealth, Stewardship of

286. Fellowship

    287. Children of God

    288. Fellowship with Christ

    289. Brotherhood of Man

    290. Covenants

    291. Friendship

292. Christian Virtues

    293. Aspiration

    294. Consecration, Devotion, Dedication

    295. Contrition

296. Compassion, Sympathy, Forbearance, Kindness
297. Courage, Bravery
298. Earnestness, Diligence, Zeal
299. Faithfulness, Fidelity, Dependability
300. Generosity, Benevolence
301. Goodness, Righteousness
302. Grace
303. Gratitude, Thanksgiving,
Praise
304. Greatness
305. Holiness, Perfection
306. Honor
307. Hospitality
308. Humility
309. Influence, Example
310. Integrity, Honesty
311. Joy, Gladness, Cheerfulness,
Optimism
312. Justice
313. Loyalty
314. Mercy
315. Obedience
316. Patience
317. Peace, Contentment, Quietness, Rest
318. Power
319. Purity, Chastity
320. Purpose
321. Resignation
322. Responsibility
323. Reverence, Awe
324. Self-denial, Self-sacrifice
325. Serenity, Calmness

326. Sincerity

327. Simplicity

328. Strength

329. Temptation

330. Conscience

331. Values, Truth

332. Little Things

333. Great Things

334. Death

335. Resurrection

336. Eternal Life

337. Kingdom of God

338. Personal Religion

339. Books of Devotion

340. Family and Home

341. Romance, Courtship

342. Betrothal

343. Marriage

344. Weddings

345. Family Altar, Family Worship

346. Grace at Table

347. Relation of Home to Church

348. Pastoral Responsibility

349. Fatherhood

350. Motherhood

351. Parental Responsibility

352. Births

353. Birthdays

354. Child Psychology

355. Child Nurture and Care

356. Home Making

357. Love

358. Loyalty

359. Happiness

360. Interests

361. Values
362. Individualism
363. Discipline
364. Education of Children
365. Relation of Home and School
366. Books for Children
367. Health
368. Relation of Home to Community
369. Child and Youth Delinquency
370. Adult Delinquency
371. Divorce
372. Home Problems
373. Recreation and Play
374. Vacation
375. Games
376. Fun
377. Age, Gerontology
378. Death in the Home
379. Funerals
380.
381.
382.
383. The Church
384. Influence of the Church
385. Relation of Church to Morals, Civilization, etc.
386. Democracy
387. Communism
388. Socialism
389. National Mores
390. Literature
391. Motion Pictures
392. Radio
393. Television

394. Relation of Church to Social Problems, Movements, Philanthropies, Humanitarianism, Relief
    395. Alcoholism
    396. Use of Narcotics
    397. Hospitals, Healing
    398. Red Cross
    399. Race Problems, Segregation
400. Relation of Church to Industry and Business
    401. Labor Movement
402. Relation of Church to Education
    403. Universities
    404. Colleges
    405. Schools
    406. Boy Scouts
    407. Girl Scouts, etc.
    408. Adult Education
    409. Sex Education
410. Relation of Church to Government, Politics, Administration of Justice
    411. The State and the Church
    412. Chaplaincy
    413. Courts
    414. Prisons and Crime
    415. Legislation
416. Relation of Church to International Affairs
    417. United Nations
    418. Diplomacy
    419. War
    420. Peace
    421.
422. Doctrine of The Church
423. Church Polity, Church Government

424. Church Doctrines
425.
426. Church Architecture
    427. Church Equipment
    428. Church Furnishings
        429. Organs
430. Ecclesiology
    431. Aesthetics, Beauty
    432. Symbolism
    433. Religious Art
434. Sabbath, Lord's Day, Sunday
435. Worship, Divine Service, Ritual, Liturgics
        436. Church Calendar, Bulletins, Programs, Orders of Service
        437. Ushering
        438. Prayers with the Choir
        439. Calls to Worship
        440. Invocations
        441. Responsive Readings
        442. Litanies
        443. Prayers, Pastoral
        444. Offertory Sentences
        445. Offertory Prayers
        446. Silence in Worship
        447. Preaching
        448. Benedictions
    449. Mid-week Service, Prayer Meeting, Family Night
    450. Religious Drama
    451. Audio-Visual Aids
    452. Aids to Worship
        453. Prayer Books
454. Sacred Music and Hymnology
    455. Hymns

456. Authors of Hymns

457. Composers of Hymns

458. Hymn Books

459. Anthems, Chants, Introits

460. Choir

461. Orchestra

462. Religious Poetry

463. Sacraments and Ordinances, Special Rituals

464. The Lord's Supper, Eucharist, Communion

465. Baptism

466. Dedication of Children

467. Reception of Members

468. Ordination

469. Installations

470. Dedication of Church Buildings, Organs, etc.

471. Solemnization of Matrimony, Wedding Services

472. Burial of Dead

473. Christian Education

474. Church School, Sunday School

475. Administration of Church School

476. Curriculum and Aids

477. Teaching

478. Methods

479. Aids

480. Vacation Church Schools

481. Adult Religious Education

482. Church Library

483. Missionary Education

484. Temperance Education

485. Theological Education

486. Bible Institutes and Bible Colleges

487. Theological Seminaries

488. Education in Sacred Music

489. Church Triumphant, Communion of Saints

490. Homiletics, Pastoral Work, Preaching

491. Ministry and Clergy

492. Preaching

493. Sermons

494. Original Sermons

495. Sermons of Others

496. Sermon Texts and Themes

497. Sermonic Literature

498. Pastoral Work

499. Ministry to Delinquents

500. Ministry to Sick

501. Ministry to Bereaved

502. Consolation

503. Pastoral Counselling

504. Church Organization and Administration

505. Responsibilities of Laymen

506. Maintenance of Church Buildings

507. Records of Church

508. Church Finance

509. Budgets

510. Financial Canvass

511. Financial Campaigns

512. Evangelism

513. Revivals, Parish Missions

514. Retreats

515. Summer Conferences and Camps

516. Institutional Work

517. Y. M. C. A.

518. Y. W. C. A.
519. Neighborhood Houses
520. Interest Clubs
521. Athletics
522. Organizations for Fellowship, Parish
Work, Welfare Work
523. General Organizations
524. Men's Organizations
525. Women's Organizations
526. Young People's Organizations
527. Boys' Organizations
528. Girls' Organizations
529. Church Publicity
530. Bulletin Board
531. Slogans for Bulletin Board
532. Sunday Calendar
533. Parish Paper
534. Newspaper Publicity
535. Statistics
536. The Rural Church
537. The City Church
538. The Suburban Church
539. Church Attendance
540.
541. Missions
542. International Missionary Organizations
543. Boards of Missions
544. Missionary Societies and Movements
545. Laymen's Missionary Movement
546. History of Missions
547. Apostolic Missions, First Century
548. Early Church Missions, Second and
Third Centuries
549. Early European Missions, Fourth
to Eighth Centuries

550. Period of the Middle Ages, Ninth to Fifteenth Centuries
551. Period of the Reformation, Sixteenth and Seventeenth Centuries
552. Period of the Early Missionary Societies, Eighteenth Century
553. Modern Missions, Nineteenth and Twentieth Centuries
554. Mission Fields, the Younger Churches, Stories, Statistics
555. India
556. Pakistan
557. Southeastern Asia
558.
559.
560.
561. China
562. Japan
563. Korea
564. Pacific Islands
565.
566.
567.
568. The Near East
569.
570.
571.
572. Africa
573.
574.
575.
576.
577. Latin America
578.
579.

580.

581.

582.

583.

584. Europe

585.

586.

587.

588.

589. Orphaned Missions

590. North America, Home Missions, National Missions

591.

592.

593.

594. City Missions

595. Unoccupied Fields

596. Church Union on Mission Fields

597. Missionary Outlook

598. Missionary Methods

599. Agricultural Missions

600. Educational Missions

601. Evangelistic Missions

602. Faith Missions

603. Medical Missions

604. Missions to Jews

605. Missions to Lepers

606. Missions to Seamen

607. Training of Missionaries

608. Missionary Leaders

609. Missionary Literature

610. History of the Christian Church

611. Greco-Roman Civilization, Preparation for Christianity

612. Jewish Life and Thought, Preparation
for Christianity
613. The Apostles
614. Apostolic Churches, First Century
615. Christianity and the Roman Empire
    616. Persecutions
    617. Martyrs
    618. Sects, Systems, Parties
    619. Heresies
    620. Early Christian Literature
    621. Church Fathers
622. Adoption of Christianity by Rome as the
State Religion
    623. Controversies
624. The Papacy
625. The Mediaeval Church
    626. Crusades
627. The Protestant Reformation, The
Protestant Revolution
    628. Humanism and the Reformation
    629. The Lutheran Reformation
    630. Anabaptists
    631. The Calvinistic Reformation
    632. The English Reformation
    633. The Reformation in Other Lands
634. The Counter-Reformation
635. Religious Wars
636. Era of Modern Denominationalism
    637. Denominational Histories
    638.
    639.
    640.
    641.
    642.
    643. Local Church History

644. Records
645. Publications
646. Lists
647. Clippings
648. Photographs
649. Letters
650.
651.
652. Denominations, Sects, Churches in All Lands
   653. Roman Catholicism
   654.
   655.
   656.
   657. Eastern Orthodox Churches
   658. Protestantism
      659. Adventist Churches
      660.
      661.
      662. Assemblies of God, Pentecostal Churches, Churches of God
      663.
      664.
      665. Baptist Churches
      666.
      667.
      668.
      669. Brethren Churches, Dunkers, etc.
      670.
      671.
      672. Christian and Missionary Alliance
      673. Christian Reformed Church in America
      674. Community Churches
      675. Congregational Churches
      676. Congregational-Christian Church

677. Disciples of Christ
678. Episcopal Churches, Protestant Episcopal
679. Evangelical and Reformed Church
680. Evangelical and United Brethren Church
681. Societies of Friends
682.
683. Holiness Churches
    684. Church of the Nazarene
    685.
    686.
687. Lutheran Churches
    688.
    689.
    690.
691. Mennonite Churches
    692.
693. Methodist Churches
    694.
    695.
    696.
    697.
    698.
699. Mission Covenant Church of America, Evangelical
700. Moravian Church
701. Plymouth Brethren
702. Presbyterian Churches
    703.
    704.
    705.
706. The Quakers
    707.
708. Reformed Church in America

709. Unitarian Church
710. Universalist Church
711.
712.
      713. Salvation Army
      714. Volunteers of America
      715. Christian Science
      716. Mormons. Latter Day Saints
717. Other Denominations, Sects, Cults, Ethical Societies
      718. Alcoholics Anonymous
      719. Moral Rearmament Movement
720. Church Co-operation, Church Union, Ecumenicity
    721. World Council of Churches
    722. National Council of the Churches of Christ in the United States of America
      723. Regional Council of Churches
      724. Local Council of Churches
    725. American Council of Christian Churches
726. Churches in Other Lands
    727. Canada
    728. England
    729. Scotland
    730. Norway
    731. Sweden
    732. Holland
    733. Australia
    734. New Zealand
    735. South Africa
    736.
    737.
    738.

739.

740.

741.

742.

743. Statistics of Denominations, etc.

744. The Year, Seasons, Days

745. Anniversaries

746. Spring

747. Summer

748. Autumn

749. Winter

750. Vacation

751. January

752. February

753. March

754. April

755. May

756. June

757. July

758. August

759. September

760. October

761. November

762. December

763. Morning

764. Evening

765. Advent

766. Christmas

767. New Year

768. Lent

769. World Day of Prayer

770. Week of Prayer

771. Youth Week

772. Youth Sunday

773. Race Relations Sunday

774. Brotherhood Sunday
775. Lincoln's Birthday
776. Day of Prayer for Students
777. Washington's Birthday
778. Holy Week
779. Palm Sunday
780. Maundy Thursday
781. Good Friday
782. Easter
783. Missionary Sunday
784. Family Week
785. Christian Home Sunday
786. Mothers' Day
787. Rural Life Sunday
788. Memorial Day
789. Ascension Day
790. Pentecost, Whitsunday
791. Commencement Sunday
792. Children's Day
793. Christian Unity Sunday
794. Trinity Sunday
795. Fathers' Day
796. Flag Day
797. Independence Day
798. Labor Sunday
799. Loyalty Sunday
800. Rally Day
801. Christian Education Week
802. World-Wide Communion Sunday
803. Laymen's Sunday
804. United Nations Week
805. World Order Day
806. All Saints' Day
807. Reformation Sunday
808. Stewardship Sunday

809. World Temperance Sunday
810. Peace Sunday
811. Election Sunday
812. Armistice Day, Veterans' Day
813. Thanksgiving Day
814. Bible Sunday
815. Forefathers' Sunday
816. Watch Night
817.
818.
819.
820. Community, National and International Life
821. Altruism
822. Atom Bomb
823. Canada
824. Capitalism
825. Care of the Aged, Gerontology
826. Church and State
827. American Citizenship
828. Civilization
829. Communism
830.
831.
832. Constitution of the United States
833. Bill of Rights
834. Declaration of Independence
835. Democracy
836.
837.
838.
839. Divorce
840. Education
841. Universities
842. Colleges
843. Public Schools

844. Religion in the Public Schools
845. Parochial Schools
846. Vocational Education
847.
848.
849. Fraternal Orders, Lodges
850.
851.
852. Gambling
853. Hospitals
854. Humane Societies, Kindness to Animals
855. Income Tax, Taxation
856. Industry
857. Labor, Labor Unions
858. Administration of Laws
859. Liberty, Freedom
860. Life, Life Expectation, etc.
861. Liquor Traffic, Drinking, Temperance
Movement
862. Luxury
863. Mentally Ill, Care of, Statistics
864. Morality, Ethics
865. Use of Narcotics
866. Nationalism
867. Patriotism
868. Peace
869. World Peace
870. Peace Movements
871. Pensions
872. Political Parties
873. The Church and Political Action
874. Poverty
875. The Press
876. Profanity
877. Progress

878. Race Relations
    879. Segregation
880. Red Cross
881. Secularism
882. Socialism
883. Social Justice
884. Social Service
885. Social Security
886. United Nations
887. War
    888. Consciencious Objectors
889. Wealth
890. Welfare
891.
892.
893.
894.
895.
896.
897.
898.
899.
900.
901. Non-Christian Religions and Philosophies
    902. Religion of Primitive Peoples, Animism, etc.
    903. Ancestor Worship
    904. Hinduism
    905. Jainism
    906. Buddhism
        907. Southern Buddhism, Hinayana
        908. Northern Buddhism, Mahayana
        909. Tibetan and Mongolian Buddhism, Lamaism
    910. Confucianism

911. Taoism
912. Shinto
913. Zoroastrianism, Parsees
914. Islam, Mohammedanism
915. Sikhism
    916. Non-Christian Cults
    917. Idolatry
    918. Superstition
    919.
    920.
    921.
    922.
    923.
    924.
    925.
    926.
    927.
    928.
929. Biographies
(Twenty numbers 930 to 949 inclusive)
950. Personal Matters, Miscellaneous
    951. Books
       952. Book Reviews
    953. Magazine Articles
    954. Hobbies
    955.
    956.
    957.
    958.
    959. Letters
       960. Personal Letters
       961. Business Letters
       962. Replies
    963. Accounts
       964. Receipts

965.

966.

967. Clippings of Personal Interest

968. Photographs

969. Income Tax

    970. Old Income Tax Returns

    971. Last Year's Income Tax Returns

    972. Current Income Tax Returns

    973. Estimates of Income Tax

974. Social Security Papers

975. Travel Notes

    976. Maps

977. Personal Writings

978. Personal Interests

979.

980.

981.

982.

983.

984. Family Interests

985.

986.

(Numbers 987 to 1000 inclusive)

TABLE III

Record of Sermons and Addresses

For the convenience of those who keep a record of their sermons, 494, talks and addresses, when and where delivered, etc.

TABLE III

Where Preached	When Preached	Remarks

TABLE III

Service Number	Sermon Number	Text	Sermon Subject

TABLE III

Service Number	Sermon Number	Text	Sermon Subject

TABLE III

Where Preached	When Preached	Remarks

TABLE III

Service Number	Sermon Number	Text	Sermon Subject

TABLE III

Where Preached	When Preached	Remarks

TABLE III

Where Preached	When Preached	Remarks